★★★★★
MLB TEAMS

Cleveland GUARDIANS

KENNY ABDO

Fly!
An Imprint of Abdo Zoom
abdobooks.com

abdobooks.com

Published by Abdo Zoom, a division of ABDO, P.O. Box 398166, Minneapolis, Minnesota 55439.

Printed in the United States of America, North Mankato, Minnesota.
102025
012026

Photo Credits: Alamy, Getty Images, Shutterstock
Production Contributors: Kenny Abdo, Jennie Forsberg, Grace Hansen
Design Contributors: Candice Keimig, Neil Klinepier

Library of Congress Control Number: 2025936770

Publisher's Cataloging-in-Publication Data

Names: Abdo, Kenny, author.
Title: Cleveland Guardians / by Kenny Abdo
Description: Minneapolis, Minnesota : Abdo Zoom, 2026 | Series: MLB teams | Includes online resources and index.
Identifiers: ISBN 9798384940166 (lib. bdg.) | ISBN 9798384940920 (ebook) | ISBN 9798384941309 (read-to-me ebook)
Subjects: LCSH: Cleveland Guardians (Baseball team)--Juvenile literature. | Baseball teams--Juvenile literature. | Professional sports--Juvenile literature. | Sports franchises--Juvenile literature. | Major League Baseball (Organization)--Juvenile literature.
Classification: DDC 796.357--dc23

Table of CONTENTS

GUARDIANS

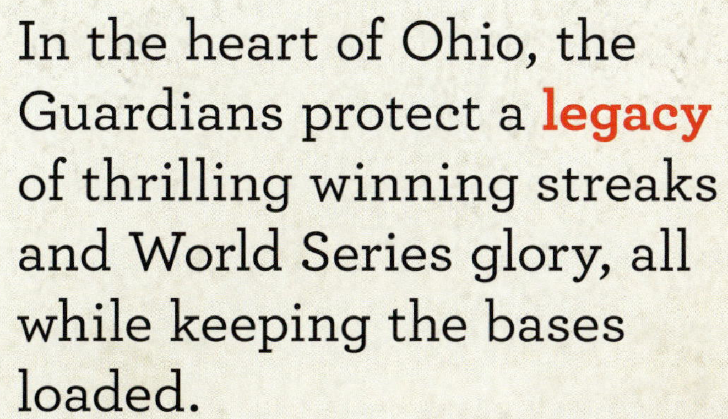

In the heart of Ohio, the Guardians protect a **legacy** of thrilling winning streaks and World Series glory, all while keeping the bases loaded.

As one of the original Major League Baseball (MLB) teams, the Guardians and its famous players honor a rich history each time they take the field.

ND FOR
LAND
GUARDIANS WIN
GUARDIANS WIN

BATTER UP!

The Guardians began as the Cleveland Blues in 1901. Cleveland was one of the eight original teams in the **American League** (**AL**). Baseball was still new, but the sport was quickly growing in popularity.

CLEVELAN

In 1915, the team got a new name and look. Just five years later, the Cleveland Indians won their first World Series by defeating the Brooklyn Robins in 1920!

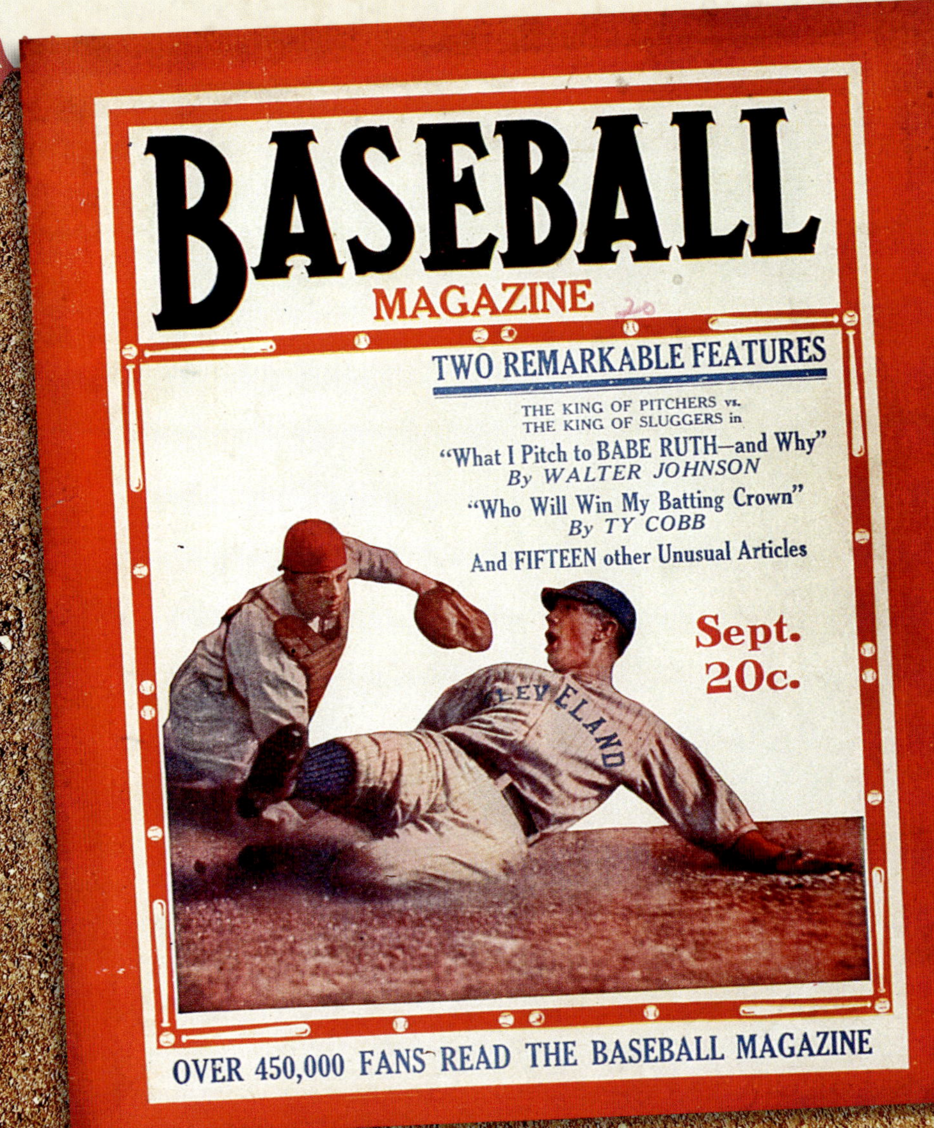
BASEBALL
MAGAZINE

TWO REMARKABLE FEATURES

THE KING OF PITCHERS vs.
THE KING OF SLUGGERS in

"What I Pitch to BABE RUTH—and Why"
By WALTER JOHNSON

"Who Will Win My Batting Crown"
By TY COBB

And FIFTEEN other Unusual Articles

Sept.
20c.

OVER 450,000 FANS READ THE BASEBALL MAGAZINE

WORLDS
CHAMPIONS

In 1948, stars Bob Feller and Larry Doby helped the team win another World Series! Gene Bearden sealed the win with a **complete game** against the Braves.

GRAND SLAMS

After many tough seasons, things began to look brighter for Cleveland in 1995. The team won 100 games and reached the World Series. Though they were bested by the Braves, it was one of the best seasons in team history.

NEED
TICKETS
FOR
GAME 7

Cleveland returned to the World Series in 1997 to face the Marlins. The series went all the way to Game 7. Ending in extra innings, the Marlins scored on a **walk-off single**. It was a sad finish for Cleveland fans.

THANK YOU!
22
NOW... ONWARD

In 2017, Cleveland made headlines with an amazing 22-game winning streak. They outscored their rivals by more than 100 runs during that stretch. Corey Kluber won the **AL Cy Young Award** that season.

In 2021, the team changed its nickname to the Guardians. “Guardians” references statues on a bridge close to the ballpark that Clevelanders know and love. It was a name that all fans could be proud of.

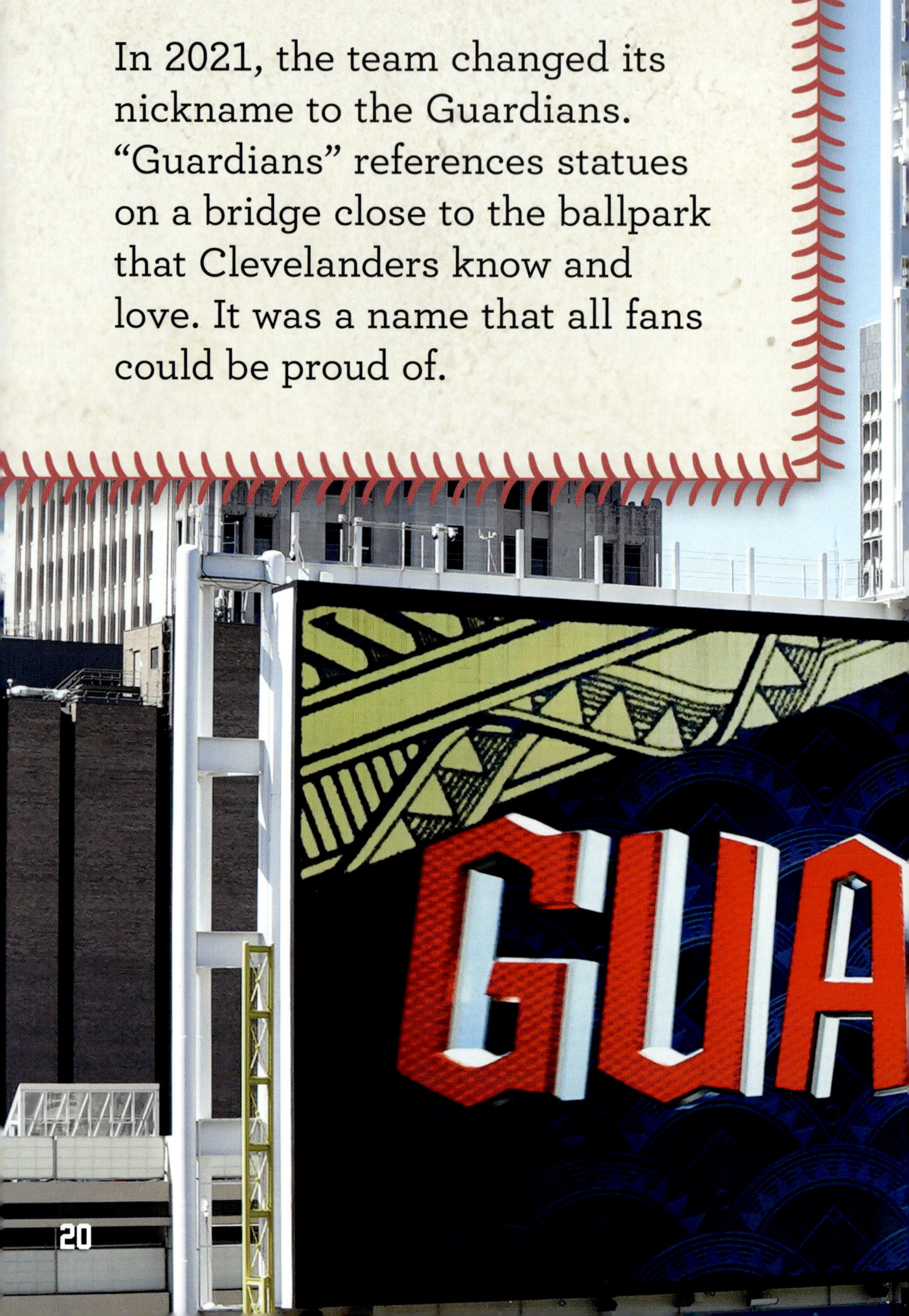

ROGRESSIVE FIELD
Guardians
RDIANS WIN
DollarBank
DollarBank

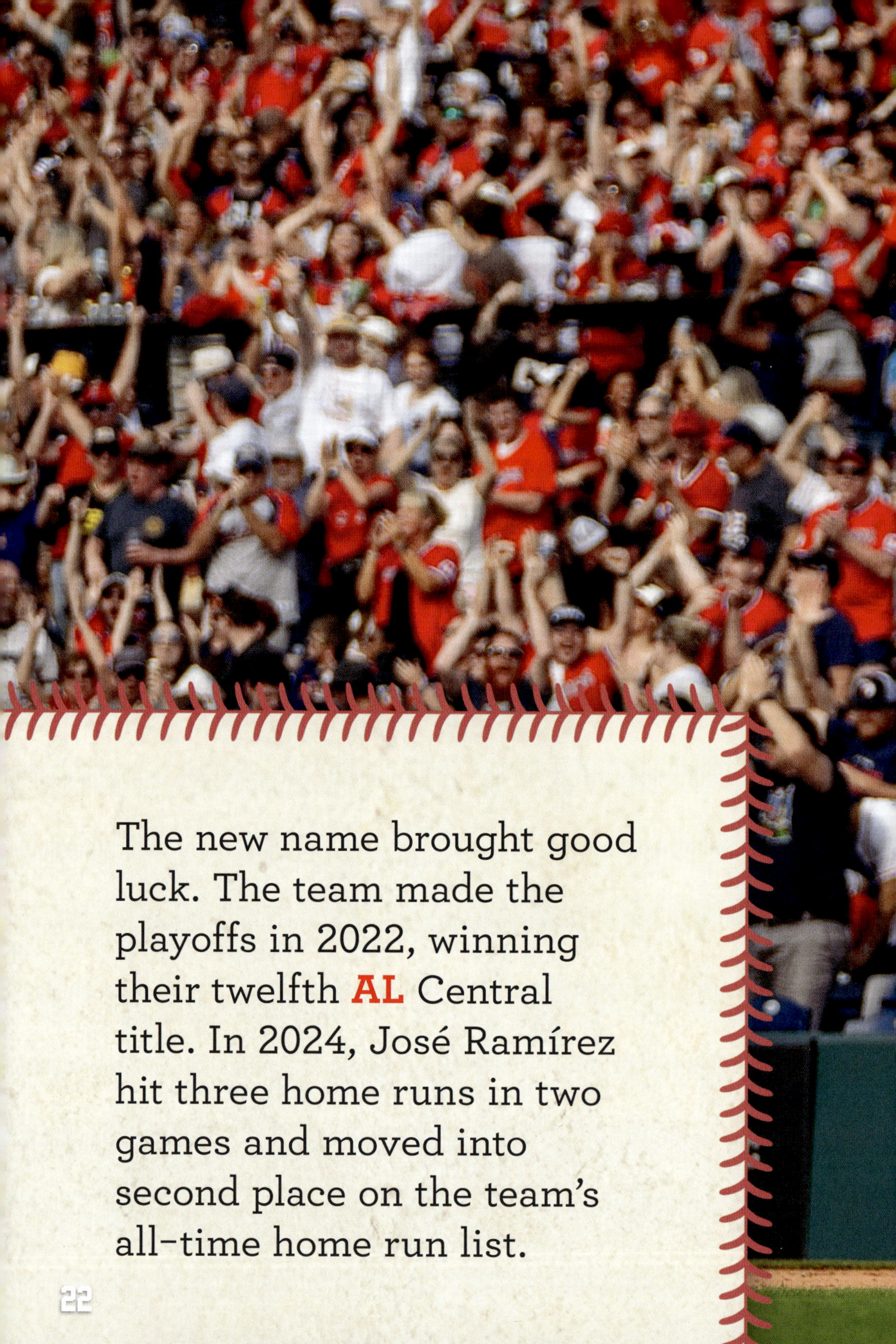

The new name brought good luck. The team made the playoffs in 2022, winning their twelfth **AL** Central title. In 2024, José Ramírez hit three home runs in two games and moved into second place on the team's all-time home run list.

In 2025, the Guardians celebrated 125 years in MLB. The team marked the **milestone** by making an incredible comeback to win the AL Central title for the second year in a row. The future was looking bright!

HALL OF FAME

From 1936 to 1956, Bob Feller spent his entire career with the Guardians. He struck out more than 2,500 batters and played in eight **All-Star Games**. Feller holds the franchise record with 266 career wins. He was named to the Baseball Hall of Fame in 1962.

Lou Boudreau was a great shortstop and a key player in the 1940s. In 1948, he won the **AL** MVP Award and led Cleveland to a World Series win. Boudreau also played in seven **All-Star Games**, including five in a row. He entered the Baseball Hall of Fame in 1970.

From 1991 to 2002, Jim Thome was the Guardians' leading slugger. He is still considered one of the greatest home-run hitters in MLB history. Thome holds the team record with 337 home runs. He was a three-time All-Star and won a Silver Slugger Award in 1996. Thome was **inducted** into the Baseball Hall of Fame in 2018.

THOME
25

GLOSSARY

All-Star Game – a yearly baseball contest where top players from the AL and the National League (NL) compete against each other.

American League (AL) – one of two 15-team leagues that make up MLB.

complete game – a game in which one pitcher pitches all innings without relief.

Cy Young Award – a trophy given to the best pitcher in the league each season.

inducted – brought in as a member.

legacy – the long-lasting impact of particular events that took place in the past.

milestone – an important event or turning point in a team's career.

walk-off single – a hit (where the batter safely reaches first base) that drives in the winning run in the bottom of the final inning.

ONLINE RESOURCES

To learn more about the Cleveland Guardians, please visit **abdobooklinks.com** or scan this QR code. These links are routinely monitored and updated to provide the most current information available.

INDEX